Money Shot

Wesleyan Poetry

Money Shot

Rae Armantrout

Wesleyan University Press

Middletown, Connecticut

Wesleyan University Press

Middletown CT 06459

www.wesleyan.edu/wespress

© 2011 by Rae Armantrout

All rights reserved

Manufactured in the United States of America

Wesleyan University Press is a member of the Green
Press Initiative. The paper used in this book meets their
minimum requirement for recycled paper.

This project is supported in part by an award
from the National Endowment for the Arts

NATIONAL
ENDOWMENT
FOR THE ARTS
A great nation
deserves great art.

Library of Congress Cataloging-in-Publication data
appear on the last printed page of this book.

5 4 3 2 1

Acknowledgments

The author thanks the editors of the following magazines
in which some of the poems appeared: *The Believer,*
the *Boston Review,* the *Chicago Review, Conjunctions,
Conjunctions Web, Court Green, Denver Quarterly, Diode,
Eleven, Gerry Mulligan, The Grand Piano 10,* the *Harvard
Advocate, Jubilat, Lana Turner, The Nation, New American
Writing,* the *New Yorker, Quarterly West,* and *Volt.*

Contents

Money Shot

Staging

1

Everything will be made new.

The precision coupling
and uncoupling,

the studied
blocking
and folding

have already begun.

2

Stillness of gauzy curtains

and the sound
of distant vacuums.

Prolonged sigh
of traffic

and the downward
curve of fronds.

The spray
of all possible paths.

Define possible.

Colony

As if
the space around
each particle were filled
with countless
virtual particles.

*

And the Lord said,

"I am aware
of weighing options,

of dither,

but the moment of decision
has always remained obscure."

*

Which one of these
do you most closely resemble?

Green stucco bungalow,

four brown gargoyles
on its flat roof.

Beehive Diva;

Rehab Idol.

*

Semi-transparent,

each

stinging jelly
is a colony.

The Given

Given potassium enough
and time,

the bougainvillea explodes

into pink
papier-mâché boxes.

*

Availability bias.

*

"The risk
of a bubble bursting

should be reflected
in the price . . ."

Money Shot

1
IndyMac:

Able to exploit pre-
existing.

Tain.

Per. In. Con.
Cyst.

2
I'm on a crowded ship
and I've been served the wrong breakfast.

This small mound
of soggy dough
is not what I ordered.

"Why don't you just *say*
what you mean?"

Why don't I?

Across

1
Wood
under an oval lake
of glass

across which
this morning
parallel wakes
appear,

gleaming bits
of skin, akin
to happiness?

2
Of course, "across"
is metaphorical.

But light is violent and weightless.

Light is the wail of atoms
pressed to touch.

It is reluctance

raised
to absolute velocity

The Agent

The time travel paradox:
each passing thought
is the thinker.

Security cameras
record each moment, but
nobody can bear to watch.

We are now convinced
that the past is populated
by automatons.

The time-traveler
is the one free agent.

When the present
goes on record,

she is thinking,
"This feels wrong!"

Prayers

1

We pray
and the resurrection happens.

Here are the young
again,

sniping and giggling,

tingly
as ringing phones.

2

All we ask
is that our thinking

sustain momentum,
identify targets.

The pressure
in my lower back
rising to be recognized
as pain.

The blue triangles
on the rug
repeating.

Coming up,
a discussion
on the uses
of torture.

The fear
that all *this*
will end.

The fear
that it won't.

Sustained

1
To come to
in the middle

of a vibrato —
an "is" —

that some soprano's

struggling
to sustain.

2
To be awake
is to discriminate

among birdcalls,
fruits, seeds,

"to work one's way,"
as they say,

"through."

3
Just now
breaking

into awareness,
falling forward,

hurtling inland
in all innocence

Working Models

A diversity noir
hit in which

a shape-shifter
and a vampire

run rival
drinking establishments.

*

Demons
handle routine tasks

once we're in the zone,

tagged
and released

into the workforce.

*

Chicks are forced to find food

grains
scattered among pebbles

while monitoring

for the appearance
of a model predator.

*

Apes can mind-read.
Studies show

what makes us human
is our tendency to point.

The Air

1
Our first gods
were cartoon characters —

quirks and *quarks* —
each dead
                    wrong,

and immortal.

2
Silence is death
and
silence is dead-air.

Give a meme
a hair-do.

Give it a split-screen.

Make it ask itself
the wrong question.

Make it eat questions
and grow long.

Service Record

If narrative
is a police report,
a woman tells her companion,
"I had woke up
at 11:03."

     *

A mourning dove walks along a low wall
with odd propriety, then flutters
to the roots of a tree nearby
where she picks up and drops
small sticks. Her chest is dusky
rose, her feet magenta.
There are intense
black circles
on her gray wings.

     *

As if any stranger
or strange thing
might serve.

     *

The only person on the street
wears brown slacks and a polo shirt.
As he walks, he slashes downward,
now and then,
with what might
almost
be a quirt.

Deviled

My dreams are cruel
children. They taunt me.

I dream I'm telling a story
the punch line of which
will involve deviled eggs.
    I'm saying
some idiot
asked me where they originated.
I found that funny
or unfair.
Launched into this anecdote,
this dream, this poem,
I'm already worried. Now I see
the pair I'm addressing
have put their heads together,
hatching something,
over the crosswords.

Measure

Mary removed it,
carefully,

from the brain case
and placed it

on the metal stand.

*

I join myself
to it, this

measured,
disinterested voice,

speaking as if
in retrospect,

as if
to another person.

*

I am not alone in this
sentence.

A bee has landed,
carefully,

on a purple tip
of lavender,

pitching in wind.

Homer

If the good is momentum,
smooth passage,
putting all this
behind you,

evil is the whirlpool,
the amplified local.

If good is the all-enduring
intention
that carries you
to the future,

evil is the present's
animal magnetism.

Wily one,
you disguise yourself
here

to appear
elsewhere
in your own person.

"If only he would come again
as he once was,"
they say.

Fuel

1

The sun on my back
like your hand

at night,
in bed,

and then again,

your hand
on my back at night

like the sun
has burned through

two-thirds of its fuel.

2

That you adorn the fallen.

That your heads
and shafts
are smooth,

cool,
a spongy marble.

That you are stock-still
and spontaneous at once.

That you *are* one

(as we always thought
we knew).

The Gift

You confuse
the image of a fungus

with the image of a dick
in my poem

(understandably)

and three days later
a strange toadstool

(white shaft, black cap,
five inches tall)

appears
between the flagstones
in our path.

We note
the invisible

web
between fence posts

in which dry leaves
are gently rocked.

Dream Life

1
Being light

green shell and flippers
in the dark ocean,

she is single
mindedness.

Then she renews herself
freely
as if shagged with pigeons.

She is tics
and junkets
perfected.

As sleep dissembles,

she enlivens creatures,
briefly,

with conviction,

as if settling
(following)

some score.

2
Briefly,
I'm surprised at the smallness
of the rooms I'm showing/
shown,

how a rumpled green bedspread

nearly fills one.

Then I'm drawn back to it,

sliding out and in

Spin

That we are composed
of dimensionless points

which nonetheless spin,

which nonetheless exist
in space,

which is a mapping
of dimensions.

*

The pundit says
the candidate's speech
hit
"all the right points,"

hit "fed-up" but "not bitter,"
hit "not hearkening back."

*

Light strikes our eyes
and we say, "Look *there!*"

Bubble Wrap

"Want to turn on CNN,
see if there've been any
disasters?"

*

In the dream,
you slip inside me.

Ponzi scheme; rhyme scheme.

The child wants his mother
to put her head
where his is, see
what he sees.

*

In the dream
inside the dream,

our new roommates
are arguing:

"These are not
Astroturf calls,

and we're all populists
now."

*

Now an engine's
single indrawn breath.

(The black hole
at the heart

of it
is taking it

all back.)

*

An immigrant
sells scorpions
of twisted electrical wire
in front of the Rite Aid.

Recording

1

It occurs to me that, in the old city, the small peculiarities
which I like to record, standing out against the familiar
chains at home, might not stand out at all or might not
seem very peculiar. Here everything is singular and
strangeness may be hard to recognize as such. Or not.
I don't know and there is no way to ask the inhabitants
about it.

2

As part of the language lesson,
I have holes cut in my forehead.

I am to learn by feel
to insert the proper keys.

I play along, though,
privately,
I still have my doubts.

Answer

a moment of stillness,
demanding an answer.

When does a moment end?

*

Starbucks prayer,
"Make morning good again."

*

Leaf shadows on pavement:

word meaning to slide
carelessly,
repeatedly,
to absentmindedly caress.

*

For I so loved the world

that I set up
my only son

to be arrested.

Day

for Gerard Manley Hopkins

"Off the brown brink."

Over smog colored
embankments,

the same split
wings
aflutter,

the exhaustive, glancing
perusal.

It flashes
but doesn't gather.

It rhymes and does not
confirm.

Eyes

After John Milton

Our light is never spent.
Is spent.

Thus have we scooped out
maceration reservoirs.

We will blaze forth
what remains
as pixels.

Great angels
fly at our behest
between towers,

along axons and dendrites,

so that things stand
as they stand

in the recruited present.

Ground

Custom content feed.

Let me tell you something personal.
As a child, I worried about quicksand.
I don't know why I mention this.
I feel no connection
to the child who had that fear,
instilled, as it was,
by '50s films about explorers,
hokey
and tainted now.

I hold out my hand.

    *

Brownian motion;
primal shudder.

The way it's hotter

to go to bed with someone
while imagining

yourself
to be another person.

Autobiography: Urn Burial

1
I could say
"authenticity"

will have been about trying
to overtake the past,

inhabit it
long enough to look around,

say "Oh,"

but the past is tricky,

holds off.

So are we really moving?

Or is this something
like the way

form appears
to chase function?

2
I might hazard that my life's course
has been somewhat unusual.
When I say that, I hear both
an eager claim
and a sentence that attempts to distance itself
by adopting the style
of a 19th-century English gentleman.
The failed authority
of such sentences is soothing,
like watching Masterpiece Theatre.

When I recount my experiences,
whatever they may have been,
I'm aware of piping tunes
I've heard before.
Or jumbled snatches of familiar tunes.
The fancy cannot cheat
for very long, can it?
In the moment of experience,
one may drown
while another looks on.

Second Person

Lemons, lanterns
hang late
into the evening.

But you are known
for your voluptuous retreat,

for leaving
your absence
on the air,

illicit, thin.

I know
you think
I wonder
if you think
of me.

This reflection
spins,

a bead on a string.

I can take it with me.

Number

1

The stirring
presence
here again,

the fresh
limpidity,

the green
dangle

which we
have always half
forgotten

or mis-
remembered as
our own.

2

To vibrate in place
for emphasis,

to trill.

3

The assumption, one
of going on,

budding off
into what

will be multiple.

4
What are later called
"functions,"

mirrored,

made into a
routine,

dazzlingly amplified
at first,

then merely
doubled,

surveilled.

Warble

1
Wordsworth's secret
freshet.

First orgasm.

Hopkins' holy
ghost.

Wordsworth's sudden
multitude

remain standing.

What burbles?
What warbles?

Sea to shining, shining

2
The angels are the old gods
with a new service
orientation.

They've put aside
their hijinks
for the greater good,

for unimpeded
transmission.

"Fear not,"
the wires sing.

Division

"Ought" meaning should

and ought,
"a cipher."

*

Each petal's
irregular

pink stripe,
candy stripe,

divides by one.

Why sweet?

Simple
as if made by kids,

reiterated
as if lacking

Soft Money

They're sexy
because they're needy,
which degrades them.

They're sexy because
they don't need you.

They're sexy because they pretend
not to need you,

but they're lying,
which degrades them.

They're beneath you
and it's hot.

They're across the border,
rhymes with dancer —

they don't need
to understand.

They're content to be
(not *mean*),

which degrades them
and is sweet.

They want to be
the thing-in-itself

and the thing-for-you —

Miss Thing —

but can't.

They want to be you,
but can't,

which is so hot.

Human

1
Rolled to the brink,
a subatomic particle
will sometimes turn away.

This is called anti-tunneling.

Or perhaps not
sometimes
but some part of it
will turn.

Does this mean
the world is human?

"Whenever a wave encounters
an abrupt change
in condition, even a change
favorable to its propagation,
some of it
will be reflected back."

"Uncertainty" predicts
that the more clearly we understand

(waves)   (particles)

the less clearly
we see
what it means to be reflected.

2
The rhythmic wince
of the artificial candles
on a dark morning
calls attention

as if calling

outside
a child yells "Mom-my!"
again and again.

Hopeless persistence
is called petulance

so that it is possible
to refer

to the petulance
of the lost

Garden

"Best wishes,"
you conclude,

and here they are —

a lineup of characters:

the loose-lipped blue hibiscus,

the flashy columbine
like a shooting star
in reverse,

the composite, scarlet verbena

made to stand
against a wall.

*

"That's nice,"
but it's the liminal,

the area between
sleep and waking up,

the border
we think we remember

between existing
and not

that we still want.

Advent

In front of the craft shop,
a small nativity,
mother, baby, sheep
made of white
and blue balloons.

             *

Sky
          god
                   girl.

Pick out the one
that doesn't belong.

             *

Something

close to nothing
                   flat
from which,

fatherless,
everything has come.

Chain Chain Chain

The argument from clean
margins.

Get plausible!

Some feed off
breakage,
some off transposition.

Minute by minute.

Tread water
with synonyms;

trade synonyms
for water.

Following

We think the gesture
must come first,

the body follows
by remaining.

*

Styrofoam cup
wrapped in clear plastic,
upside down at dawn.

Rosette articulated
by the gray plump

tongues
of a succulent.

*

We think things moving in tandem
are parts
of some larger being.

We think
things coming in order
move in tandem.

Daybreak and nightfall
are parts
of some larger being —

someone perfect

and impervious
to grief.

Spooks

1

The known world:

the familiar hitch
in the piroshki lady's step
as she lugs pastries
between seemingly empty houses.

"Lady"
as relic.

2

The sense
that the flip side
can be read
instantaneously
is one kind
of spookiness;

the other
is the sense
of an occluded bulk
or "mass"
beyond the surface
meaning.

With

It's well
that things should stir
inconsequentially
around me
like this
patina of shadow,
flicker, whisper,
so that
I can be still.

*

I write things down
to show others
later
or to show myself
that I am not alone with
my experience.

*

"With"
is the word that
comes to mind,
but it's not
the right word here.

Outage

1
We like to think
that the mind
controls the body.

We send the body on a mission.

We don't feel the body,
but we receive conflicting reports.

The body is catching flak
or flies.

The body is sprouting grapefruit.

The body is under-
performing in heavy
trading.

2
Reception is spotty.

Someone "just like me"
is born
in the future
and I don't feel a thing?

Like only goes so far.

Border Perfection

1
The days are shorter, but
the light seems to stretch out,

to hark
from a long way off.

Horizons
snap into focus,

while shadows
are distended, smudged.

It's happening again;
we take

discrepancies
for openings.

2
The sign
that the guy behind me

in the "border protection" line
is demented

is his impatience,

the way he asks
again and again

what we're waiting for

Duration

Those flurries
of small pecks

my mother called
leaky faucet kisses.

Late sun winks
from a power line

beyond the neighbor's tree.
In heaven,

where repetition's
not boring —

Silver whistles
of blackbirds

needle
the daylong day.

We're still
on the air,

still on the air,
they say

Cancellation

The idea that,
if I say it well enough,
fear
will be gone.

If I say it well enough
to make you believe

The idea that,
if you believe me,
our two beliefs
will cancel one another out.

*

In the departure gate,
the bag atop her bag spells
"Paradise" . . .

Paranormal.   Parable.

Syllable as passenger.

*

A woman on a cell phone tries:

"Are you annoyed?"

"Mom seemed . . .

good."

*

Last night, suddenly,
my head or the room
was spinning.

Now the airline's name
rises to the top
of the screen and
disappears.

Procedures

The palm tree exposes
a large number
of loose, carved spines

out of pleasure?

Boredom?

    *

To start over
in the carved moment
is to take cover.

    *

A solid short woman
in a pink wool suit

proceeds –
anxiously?   doggedly?

alone

up a sidewalk
laid down for her.

(We don't believe it.)

    *

There are two kinds
of choices,

pirate sources say:

unconscious
and desperate.

The Vesicle

1
To our amazement,
when fed on fatty acid,

the vesicle
did not simply grow,

it extended itself
into a filament.

Now the king's youngest daughter said,

"I wish I had
something like that," —

and the whole vesicle
transformed

into a slender tube
which was quite delicate.

2
Monks
mimed one another's
squiggles

carefully
by candlelight

as if they thought
creation trailed something,

as if they knew
creation looked like this

from what is
always

the outside.

Errands

The old
to-and-fro

is newly cloaked
in purpose.

There's a jumble
of hair and teeth

under the bedclothes
in the forest.

"The better to eat you with,"
it says

and nibbles us
until we laugh.

     *

An ax-man
comes to help.

     *

"To, To,"
birds cheep

to greet
whatever has come up.

"To, To"

Midnight

1
The radio is on
to praise-accuse us

of being the heartless
cardsharp,

each "damned
good." Alone

in our cars.

2
I still want
something moving

to hold my attention
fast. Hold it

briefly.

Paragraph

Record breaking *Thriller*
dance attempt.

*

Wolfman Jack style
DJ in the video game says,
"This is Wasteland Radio

and we're here for *you*."

*

You are *here*

maintaining detente
between the voices
in your head.

Immediacy is retro,
says Lytle.

*

Nostalgic/futuristic
scene in which

we can read the code —

green
flowing algorithms.

We can almost
slip right in.

The Hang

It's important to articulate
the original,

hurtful,
blurred composite.

Frames should be viewed
sequentially,

in time —
gaps

in the clouds.

Blue shapes

on their way

somewhere?

The slow parade.

It's possible
to get the hang.

Vest

Now the horizon
is pale blue.

We grab at it
spasmodically

with two
bags in our chests.

*

If we can inhale/
exhale with perfect

regularity,
it will seem

like we don't need
air at all,

but, rather,
are caught up

in a simple rhythm,
want to hear it out.

Perhaps a movement
so continuous

is not
really an act,

but a braided
strand —

a waterfall.

*

Blow into the tube
to inflate the

Exact

Quick, before you die,
describe

the exact shade
of this hotel carpet.

What is the meaning
of the irregular, yellow

spheres, some
hollow,

gathered in patches
on this bedspread?

If you love me,
worship

the objects
I have caused

to represent me
in my absence.

*

Over and over
tiers

of houses spill
pleasantly

down that hillside.
It

might be possible
to count occurrences.

The Deal

I knew immediately that I could fall asleep if I accepted the
substitute. I must trade what I thought I knew for this face
— round, small-featured, and in early middle-age. Once
I accepted the offer, unprepossessing as it may have been,
I could be possessed. Sleep is the future, a dark tunnel
streaked with red shift. There events move forward. I could
enter it if I would say this face belonged to someone, a
suspect, maybe, or a private dick, instead of questioning,
"Why this?"

Concerning

A woman dangles her key ring
in front of the baby on her lap
as if he were a cat —

to keep him from crying.

*

I look away before,

"whatever *concerns* may mean,
an event

always concerns a point
in a situation,"

before the gyre
is a floating island

of plastic debris
the size of the United States

adrift in the Pacific.

*

You

single Q-tip

afloat

in the remaining oil

in an otherwise empty

herring tin —

you

have an air

of mystery

Objection

Thanks to the Blankety-Blank,
packets can pop out

of empty space.
So a neutrino

can pluck a W
boson

from the blank
and pass it on.

*

A man shoves books into mailers
each morning, in a happy rush,
imagining the pleasure
of his customers,
the praise
they may post
on Amazon.

*

I shut my eyes, not thinking,
feeling bursts

of irritation,
pulses behind closed

lids, each
flicker

an objection
without object.

*

Unite my heart,
beaten small

in the secret place
of thunder.

Ends Meet

1
Could be
time is practice,

balance,

the action
executed in the mind
before and after.

Where does mind end?

2
We mark a break
with what has come before,

come through the door,

down the hatch.

Not a *clean* break
exactly.

3
Our life was rehearsal,
Mother almost said

so that we believed
we would escort her

to the future
where she could be happy.

Over

1
Love wants you
to grow, be
otherwise,
and to stay
within range.

Love wants you
to do well,
win out,
and now, all day,
you are finishing this level.

2
A voice
on the air says,

"We have very few
cards
left to play.

We are going to need
to start juggling

now   *if*

we want to get out
of this hole."

3
Outside the box,

a bird's metallic voice
drops straight

through the blaze

Sway

Caught up
in the leaf,

entranced,

the carbon atom
gets a life —

but whose life is it?

*

A slender whirlpool,

momentary poppy,

sways
over a drain.

Forget her.

She doesn't love you.

You will never have
such grace.

Along

A scatter
of cold cases

makes two
separate strings.

Rival news hours
mime discovery.

    *

For so long
we've been practicing —

unwrapping
our surprise.

    *

In heaven
the soul is sheltered

from the expanse
of time.

It contracts
to a point
of light

or spreads out
"all along"
like a wave.

    *

The real is what
can't escape

Hopscotch

We would run ahead, stop, spin around

to see where we had been
mistaken.

Or we sat apart
together, bemused
by the running, the shouting.

At the pension office too,
we were laughing
spies.

With a glance
I moved your eyes

to a fat old woman
in pigtails,

her face stamped
by disappointment.

I said nothing.

This Is

1

"If you can read this,
you're too close."

This has been specially
handcrafted in Mexico.

"Hi, you'll do"
on a tee-shirt

made by young girls
in Thailand?

America poses
in whose mirror?

Irascible.

Insouciant.

2

This is a five star trance.

To have this vantage
from the cliff's edge,

to get drunk on indifference,

to stare

at a bright succession
of crests

raised from nothing
and flattened.

Money Talks

1
Money is talking
to itself again

in this season's
bondage
and safari look,

its closeout camouflage.

Hit the refresh button
and this is what you get,

money pretending
that its hands are tied.

2
On a billboard by the 880,

money admonishes,
"Shut up and play."

Long Green

Such naked spines
and vertebrae —

convincing parallels —

upright, separated

by a few inches
of clay.

Such earnest, green
gentlemen,

such stalwarts
jouncing

in the intermittent
wind.

*

"Idea laundering

exists primarily

to produce a state

of equilibrium."

*

All night
the sea coughs up

green strands,

cold boluses

and swallows them
back in

Win

Card in the mail:

"Win a free
cremation."

*

On the tabletop,
a scatter,

grains of salt
(sugar?)

aglow.

*

It works for me.

Gracious wood grain
supplying

what I like best:

an illusion
of passage.

Real Article

Everything I know
is something I've repeated.

Lazy horn solo
tries to wander off,
but can't,

or does,
and we don't notice.

Veterans Day flags
lap idly
at their poles.

The day is warm.
"The."

About the Author

Rae Armantout is a professor of writing and literature at the
University of California, San Diego, and the author of eleven
books of poetry, most recently *Versed* (2009), winner of the
Pulitzer Prize.

LIBRARY OF CONGRESS CATALOGING-IN-PUBLICATION DATA

Armantrout, Rae, 1947–

Money shot / Rae Armantrout.

   p. cm. — (Wesleyan poetry)

ISBN 978-0-8195-7130-4 (cloth : alk. paper)

I. Title.

PS3551.R455M66 2011

811'54--dc22   2010036223